Sports and My Body

Soccer

Charlotte Guillain

Heinemann Library
Chicago, Illinois

www.capstonepub.com
Visit our website to find out more information about Heinemann-Raintree books.

To order:
☎ Phone 800-747-4992
💻 Visit www.capstonepub.com
to browse our catalog and order online.

© 2009 Raintree
an imprint of Capstone Global Library, LLC
Chicago, Illinois

Customer Service: 888-454-2279

Visit our website at www.heinemannraintree.com

Edited by Siân Smith, Rebecca Rissman, and Charlotte Guillain
Designed by Joanna Hinton-Malivoire
Picture research by Ruth Blair
Production by Duncan Gilbert

Originated by Chroma Graphics (Overseas) Pte. Ltd
Printed and bound in the United States of America in North Mankato, Minnesota. 042014 008162RP

16 15 14
10 9 8 7 6 5 4

Library of Congress Cataloging-in-Publication
Guillain, Charlotte.
  Soccer / Charlotte Guillain.
    p. cm. -- (Sports and my body)
  Includes bibliographical references and index.
  ISBN 978-1-4329-3456-9 (hc) -- ISBN 978-1-4329-3461-3 (pb) 1. Soccer--Juvenile literature. I. Title.
  GV943.25.G85 2008
  796.334--dc22
                        2009007082

Acknowledgments
The author and publishers are grateful to the following for permission to reproduce copyright material: Alamy p. **15** (© Christina Ferrin); Corbis pp. **4** (Christian Liewig), **5** (Marcus Brandt/dpa), **6** (Kevin Dodge), **8** (Ned Frisk Photography), **9** (Jim Cummins), **11** (Fancy/Veer), **17** (MM Productions), **19** (Jon Feingersh/zefa), **20** (Wolfgang Flamisch/zefa), **23** (MM Productions), **23** (Marcus Brandt/dpa); Getty Images pp. **10** (Amy Guip/Photographer's Choice), **12** (Anita van Zyl/Gallo Images), **16** (Andrew Olney/Stone), **18**, **23** (Brad Wilson); iStockphoto pp. **22**, **22**, **22**, **14** (© Matthew Ragen), **22**, **23** (© Oktay Ortakcioglu); Photolibrary p. **21** (Monkey Business Images Ltd); p. **7**, **23** (© Digital Vision); Science Photo Library pp. **13**, **23** (GUSTOIMAGES).

Cover photograph of a football being kicked reproduced with permission of Punchstock/Brand X Pictures. Back cover images reproduced with permission of iStockphoto: 1. whistle; 2. shin pads (© Oktay Ortakcioglu).

Every effort has been made to contact copyright holders of material reproduced in this book. Any omissions will be rectified in subsequent printings if notice is given to the publishers.

Contents

Some words are shown in bold, **like this**. You can find them in the glossary on page 23.

What Is Soccer?

Soccer is a game we play with a ball. People play soccer all around the world.

Some people play soccer for a team. Some people play soccer with their friends.

How Do I Learn to Play Soccer?

You can learn to play soccer in a park or a playground. All you need is a ball and a few friends.

You might play soccer at school or in a club. A **coach** or teacher will help you.

How Do I Use My Legs and Feet?

You use your legs to run when you play soccer. You use your feet to **control** the ball.

You use your feet to steal the ball
from other players. You kick the ball
with your feet. Sometimes you can
score a goal.

How Do I Use My Arms and Hands?

Goalkeepers, or goalies, use their hands to save, or catch, the ball. They can stop other players from scoring a goal.

Other players can throw the ball back from the edge of the field.

Otherwise they should not touch the ball with their hands when they play.

How Do I Use the Rest of My Body?

You can use your head to **control** the ball. You can also use your head to pass the ball to another player, or even to shoot the ball into the goal.

You can also use your chest to control the ball. It is easier to keep control of the ball if you watch it closely.

What Happens to My Body When I Play Soccer?

When you play soccer you will start to feel warm and sweaty. You will also feel thirsty.

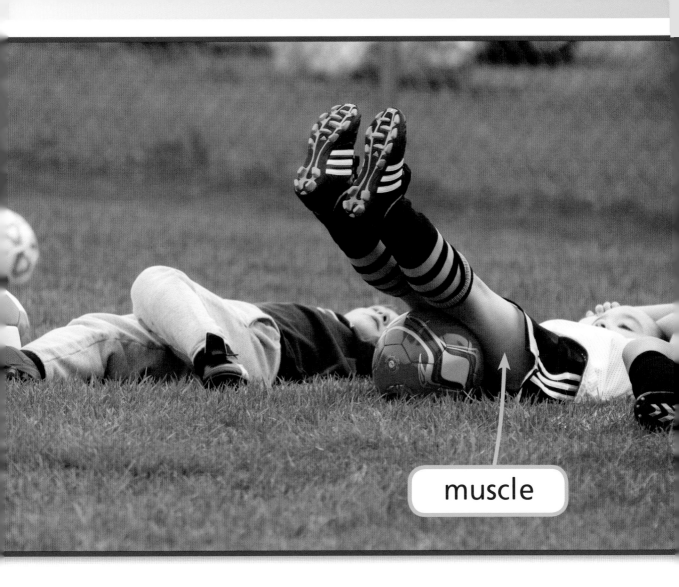

muscle

Your heart will beat faster and you will breathe more quickly. The **muscles** in your legs might ache and feel tired.

How Does It Feel to Play Soccer?

It is great to be part of a team.
It is a good feeling when you play
a game together.

You can make new friends when you play soccer. It is fun to play together outside in the fresh air.

How Do I Stay Safe Playing Soccer?

You should always warm up before you play soccer. This gets your **muscles** ready to play and keeps you from getting hurt. You can also wear **shin guards** to stay safe.

You should always follow the rules and listen to your **coach** or the **referee**. They want to keep the players safe.

Does Playing Soccer Make Me Healthy?

Soccer is good exercise and will help to keep you fit. You should also eat healthy food and drink plenty of water.

To stay healthy you need to get plenty of rest. Then you can have fun in many different ways.

Soccer Equipment

soccer ball

soccer cleats

shin guards

whistle

Glossary

 **coach** trainer. A coach helps people to learn and become better at something.

 **control** making something move the way you want it to

 **muscle** part of your body that helps you to move. Exercise can make muscles bigger and stronger.

 **referee** person in charge of making sure that players in a game follow the rules

 **shin guard** safety equipment players wear to protect their shins. Your shin is the front part of your leg below the knee.

Index

Find Out More

http://funschool.kaboose.com/fun-blaster/soccer/
This Website has games to help you learn about soccer.
You can also learn about the history of soccer.

www.usyouthsoccer.org
At this Youth Soccer Website, you can learn about local
soccer programs and see videos of different skills.